Algernon and his Amazing Aeroplane

Written and
Illustrated
by
Mark Perkins

Algernon and his Amazing Aeroplane. Copyright © 2024 Mark Perkins

All rights reserved.
No part of this book can be reproduced in any form or by written, electronic or mechanical, including photocopying, recording, or by any information retrieval system without written permission in writing by the author. The only exception is by a reviewer, who may quote short excerpts in a review.

Book & Cover design by Mark Perkins.
To see more of Hiccup and his teddy-bear friends, visit the website;
http://www.blueskiesartwork.co.uk/
Currently suitable for desktop and laptop computers only.

Published by Blue Skies Artwork.
Printed in the United Kingdom.
This book is a work of fiction. Names, characters, places and incidents are products of the author's imagination and used fictitiously. Any resemblance to actual persons is entirely coincidental. Although every precaution has been taken in the preparation of this book, the publisher and author assume no responsibility for errors or omissions. Neither is any liability assumed for damages resulting from the use of information contained herein.

ISBN - 9798335247474

Algernon and his Amazing Aeroplane

Algernon and Hiccup are two of the characters in an alphabet of Teddy Bears called the "AlphaBetaBears."

We have a collection of Teddy Bears which we have in the nursery for when the grandchildren come to visit. For a long time the bears asked me to draw them and it suddenly dawned on me that there are enough of them, with names which cover every letter of the alphabet. Happily I agreed when they made that request and this is actually the first book of the stories for children aged 3 to 8.
Bruno will be the next teddy-bear to make his appearance when Algernon sends Hiccup to Brazil.

Hiccup was furious when he was missed from the initial book of Teddy Bears; to keep him happy he will now appear in every story ... he is such a naughty bear! On the inside back cover you can meet all the bears who make up "ALPHABETABEARS."

Written and Illustrated by
Mark Perkins

Hello everyone

Algernon and his Amazing Aeroplane

This is one of the 26 books about the Alphabetabears.
At the back of the book you will find a list of all the book titles with pictures of the 26 teddy-bears (plus Hiccup of course)

"Another hot African day ahead." Algernon thought to himself.
"I wish I could share this beautiful sunshine with one of my friends." he said aloud, hoping someone might hear him and join him under his arch which was made out of wooden building blocks. He was very proud of his skills in making things.
As he sat and listened to the gentle sounds of insects in the grassland, he heard a new sound which made him really sit up and listen.
He was sure it was the sound of an aeroplane.
He was wrong. Appearing ahead of him was a small airship and he could even see the person flying it.
A smile broke out over Algernon's face.
Someone had heard him.

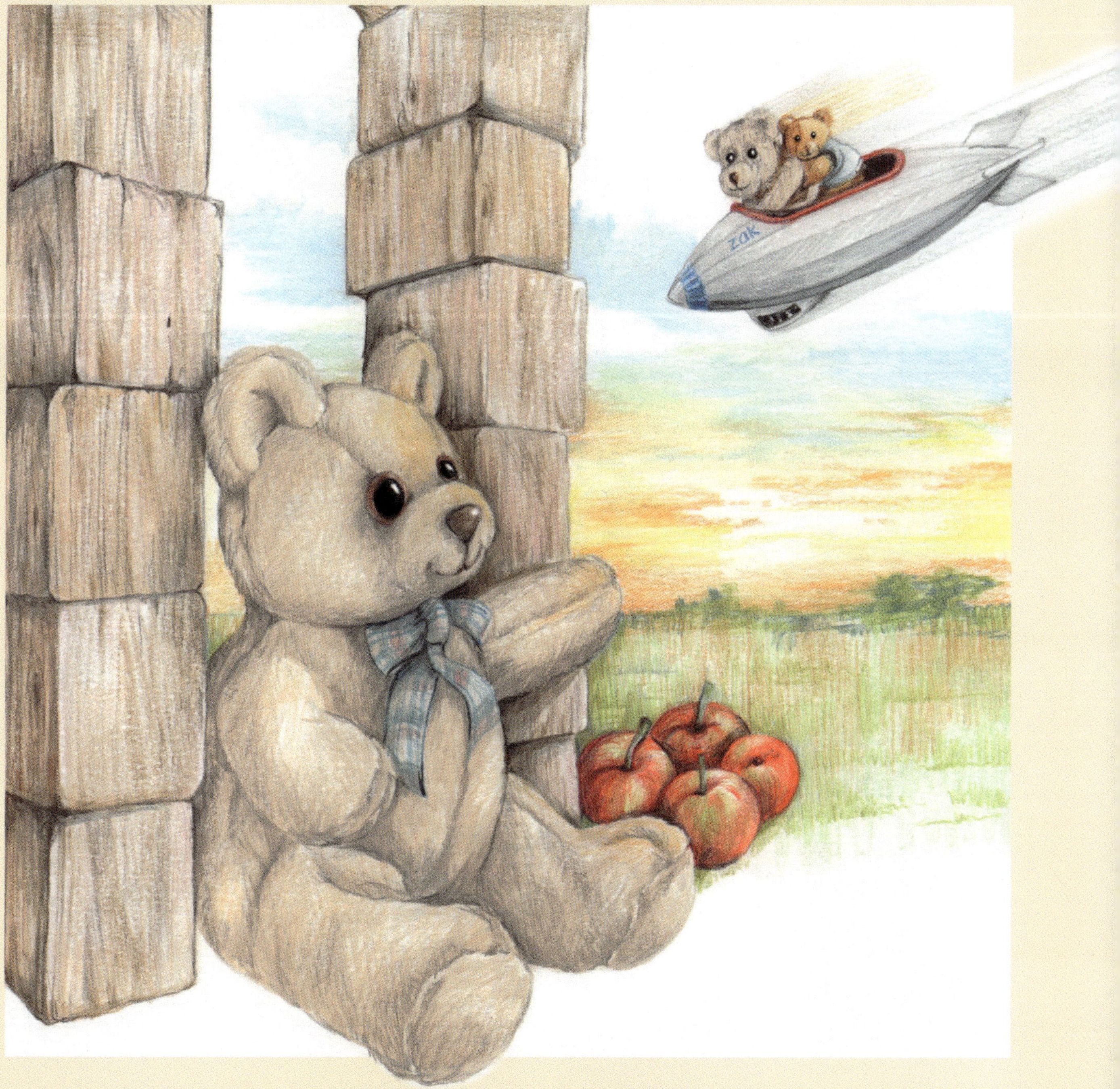
zak

Algernon watched carefully as the little airship landed on the grass.
His face lit up when he saw an old teddy-bear friend climb out – it was Zak; followed by a small teddy-bear who Algernon didn't know.
The two 'airmen' climbed out of the airship and ran across the grass to meet Algernon.
"I thought it might be you Zak. Nice airship, by the way!" Algernon greeted them.
"It is lovely to see you." he continued. "Who is this?" he added pointing to the very small bear but also looking very puzzled.
"Algernon, this is Hiccup." Zak replied. "He has been having adventures in my airship."
"Oh, I have and loved it. It's nice to see you again Algernon."

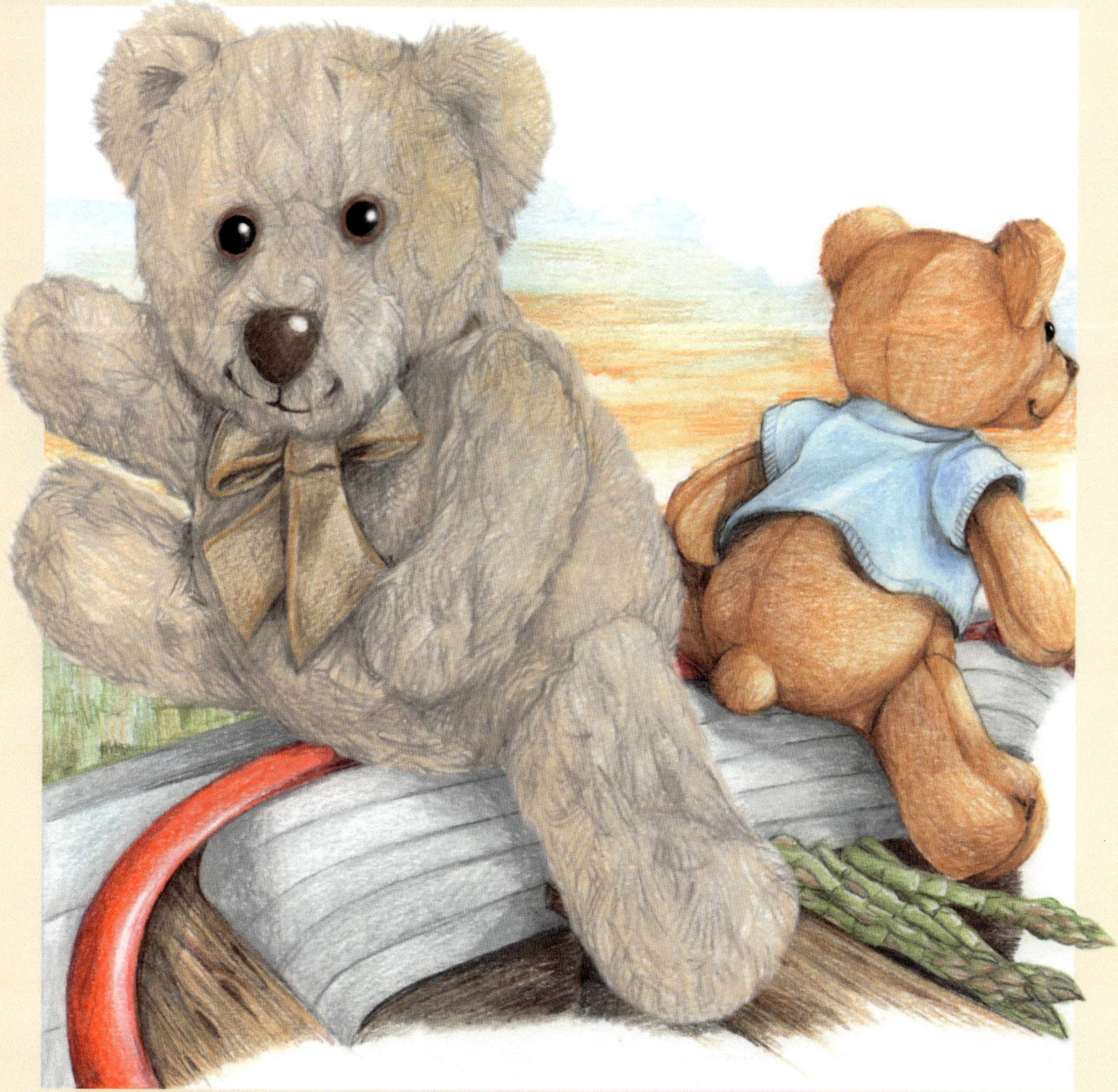

Algernon looked even more puzzled.
"What did you mean by 'again'?" he asked Hiccup.
"Well the adventures keep recurring, don't you remember meeting me before?"
Hiccup could see that Algernon was really puzzled now and he could see that Algernon was having second thoughts.
"No, I'm not certain that I do" replied Algernon.
"It's like being in a dream," explained Hiccup.
"I recall bits but not everything. I do remember you had an aeroplane. Do you still have it?"
The delighted Algernon answered quickly. "I do have it, and I think I remember you liked flying?"
"I certainly do, and I adored flying in Zak's airship." He turned to Algernon and whispered,, "It's actually a Zeppelin, you know?"
" 'A' for Airship and Aeroplane", and 'Z' is for Zeppelin. The two bears said at the same time.

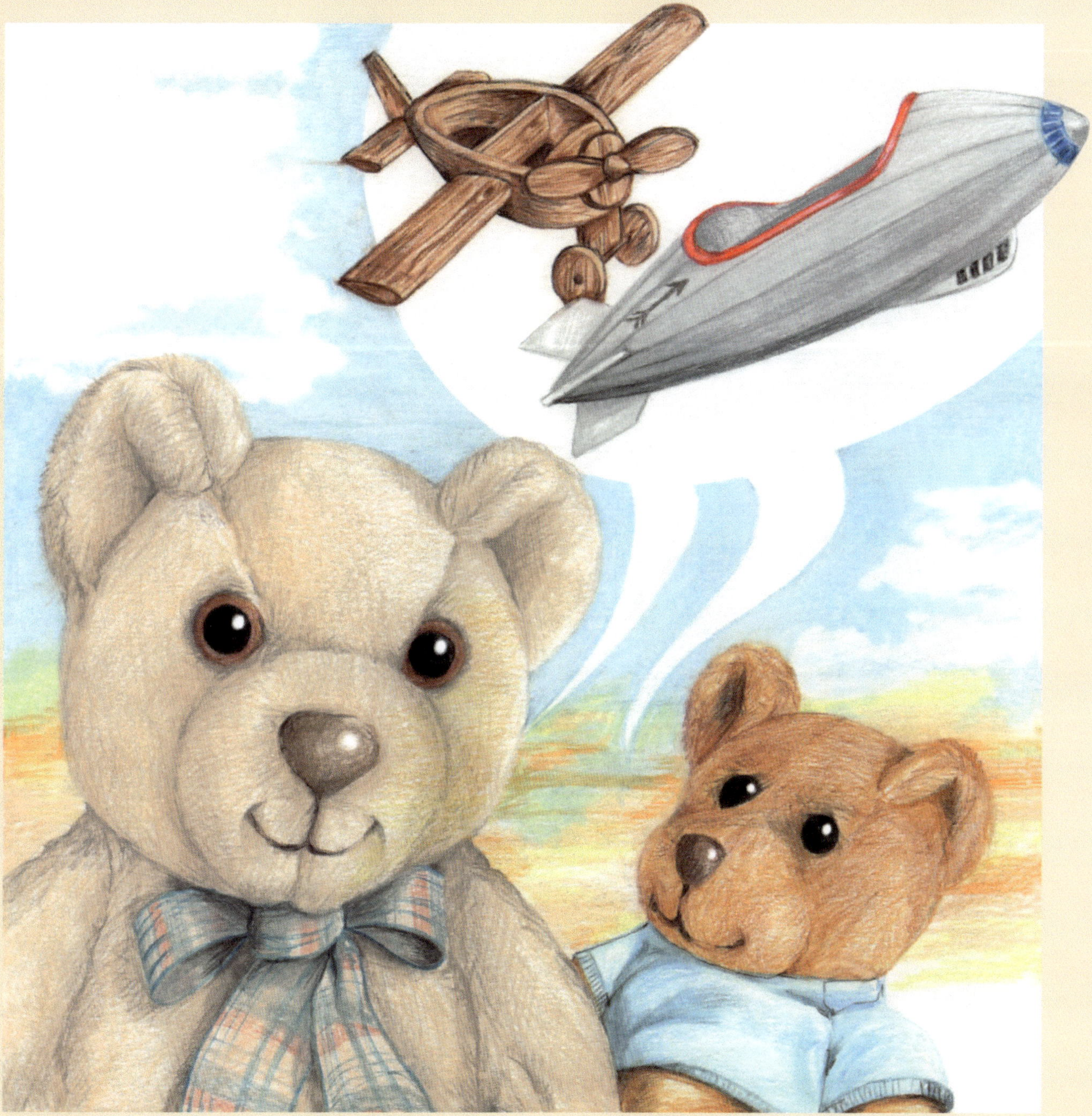

By this time, Zak felt he had helped enough and said his 'Goodbyes', climbed into the airship and took off, zooming up and away.
"Where did he go?" asked a shocked Algernon.
"Back through the big Zipper in the sky of course." replied Hiccup. "In the same way we arrived here at the start of the alphabet."
Algernon knew nothing about the zipper in the sky.
"That must be your magic, Hiccup." he said.

...where did he go?

Hiccup turned to Algernon again and asked politely.
"Could we fly in your aeroplane please?"
"I was about to suggest that Hiccup." He knew that he was just beginning to remember Hiccup.
Hiccup thought hard and then asked Algernon the question that had been troubling him.
"Is your aeroplane still magical?" He had to ask as all his recent adventures had magic attached to them.
The smiling Algernon agreed that the aeroplane did have some magic built into it.
"It's my Amazing Aeroplane!" he added. "My wooden archway is quite magical too, as you will soon discover. It can change size and lets anyone pass through to go anywhere."
The teddy-bears clambered into Algernon's aeroplane.
"Sit tight and hold onto me." Algernon told Hiccup. The aeroplane accelerated forward, turned on its side and shot through the huge archway towards a bright red African sky.

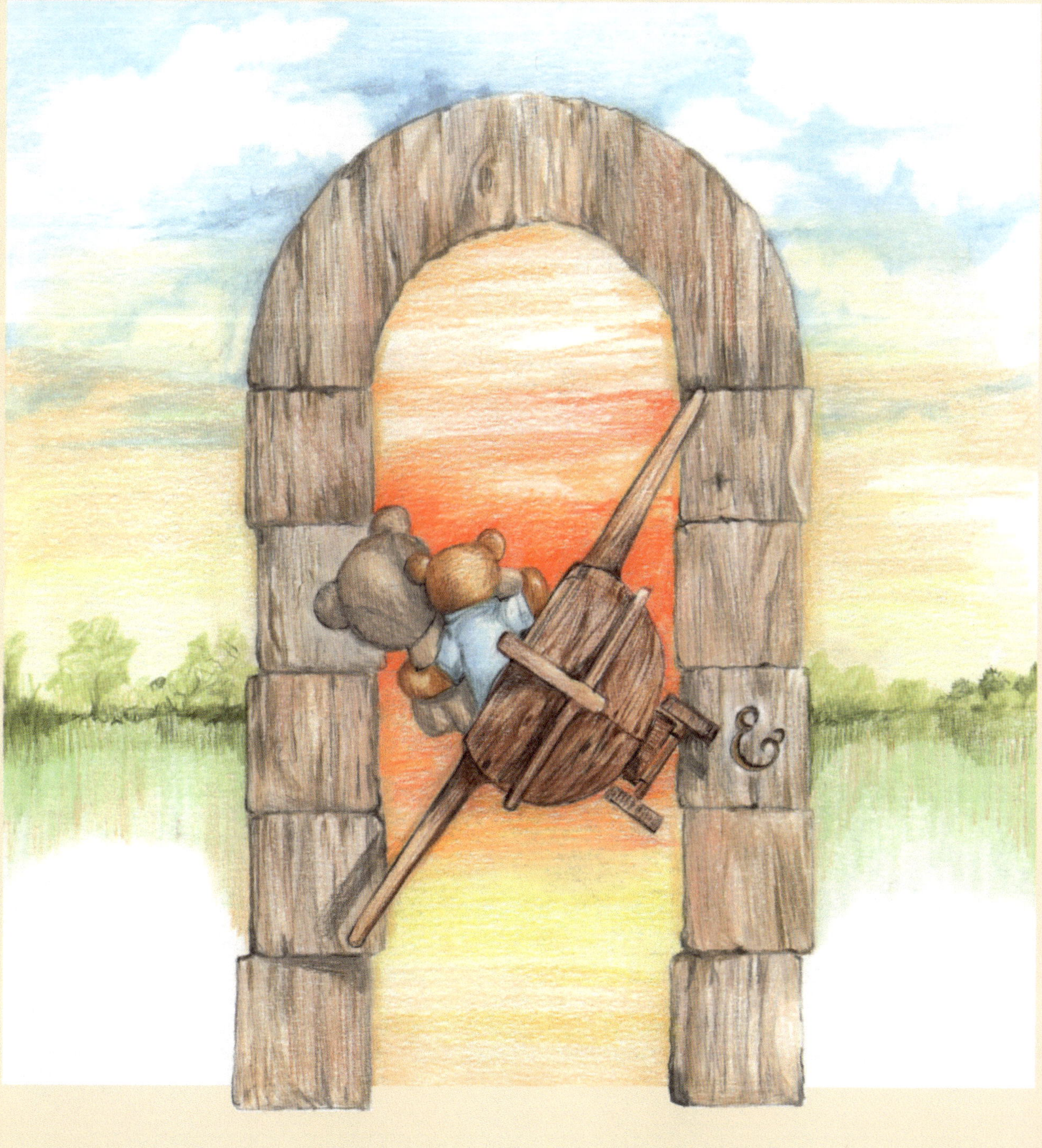

Hiccup leaned towards Algernon and shouted into the wind, just loud enough for Algernon to hear.
"Where are you taking me this time?"
"It's not my choice, the amazing aeroplane decides that, but I can see from the aeroplane's atlas that we are heading for South Africa and the game parks for animals."
Soon the aeroplane began to land amongst the grasses of a game park, Hiccup jumped up in excitement.
"There is Khamsin!" he was pointing to a lion in the long grass.
A friendly-looking lion, very friendly in fact, approached them and was soon chatting with Hiccup. An amazed Algernon appeared happy to see Hiccup enjoying himself so much. Hiccup explained that he had met Khamsin when he was with Katy, another of the Alphabetabears.
"We are old friends." Hiccup explained.

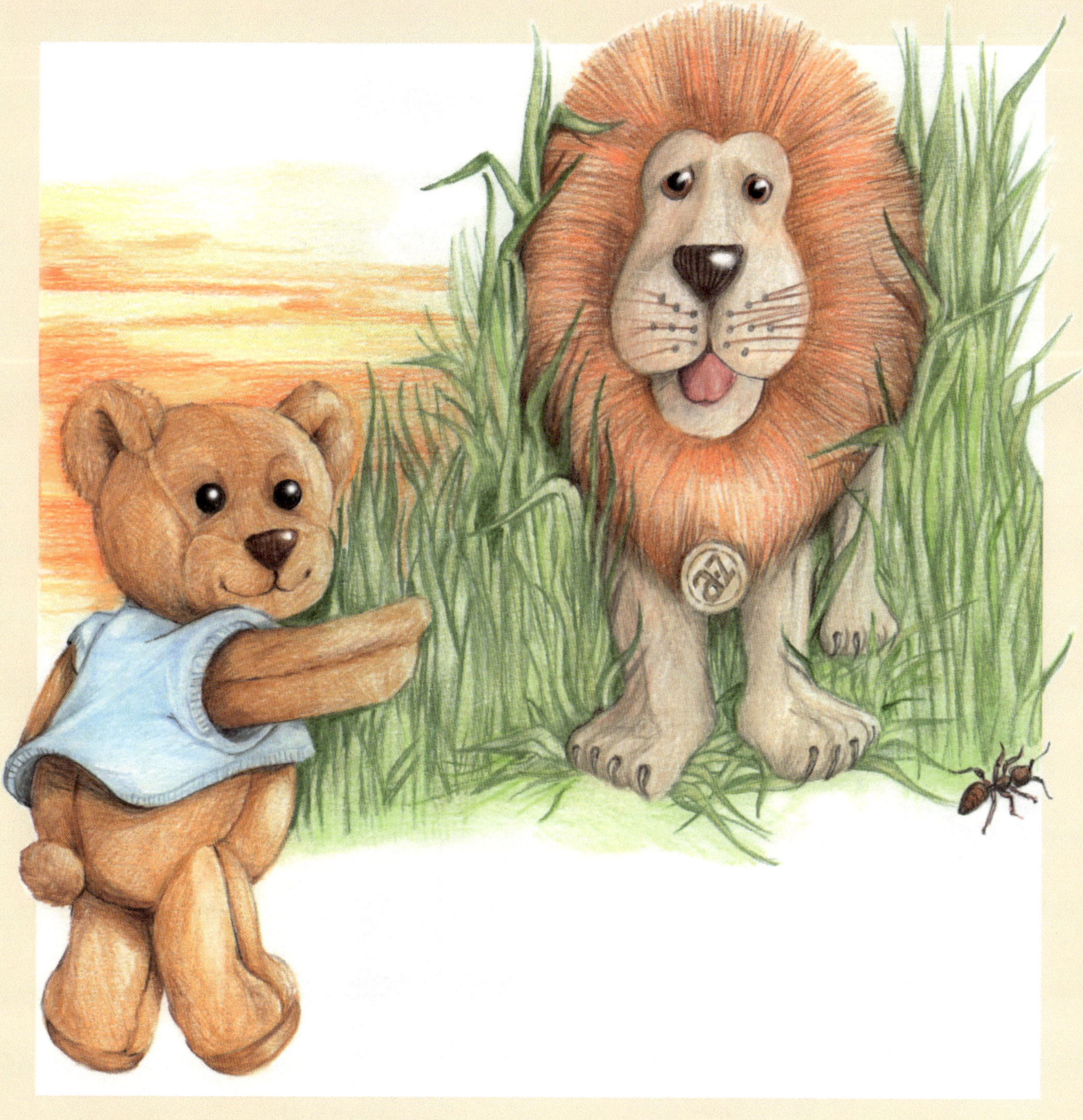

It was Algernon who was alarmed by a truck-load of human sightseers, also exploring the grasslands of South Africa.
An anxious Algernon told Hiccup and Khamsin to be careful as their truck approached. That didn't worry them, humans threw food for Khamsin and they didn't worry either. It was when they began to take an interest in Hiccup that the friends were worried ... the visitors obviously thought Hiccup was one of the wild game animals of Africa. Khamsin felt he should leave so he turned, said 'Goodbye' quickly and disappeared in the tall grass. "Quick Hiccup, hop in the aeroplane and we'll get away." Algernon shouted to him. He flew the aeroplane fast with Hiccup running to keep up. Hiccup leaped, caught hold of the aeroplane's tethering rope and held tight. Algernon steered the aeroplane through the archway, on its side, with little Hiccup hanging on acrobatically behind.

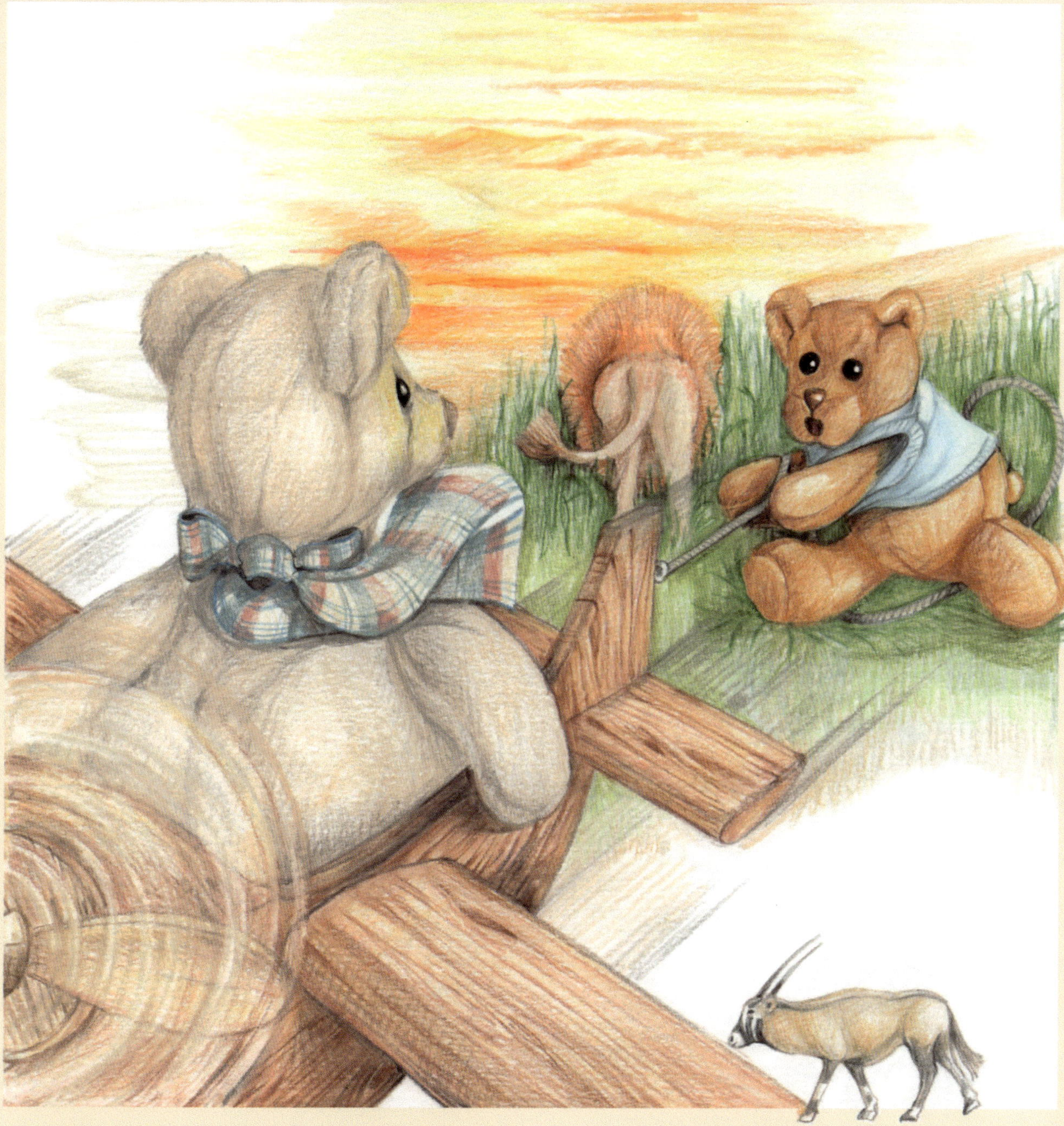

Hiccup had to hold onto the tethering rope very tightly and it was hard to talk with the wind whistling past him.
"This is turning out to be another of my awful adventures." he shouted loudly hoping Algernon could hear him.
"Oh I think you need a little adventure in your life." Algernon shouted back.
"But not as like this." Hiccup replied.
"Where are we going now?" Hiccup shouted again.
"We are going to be heading northwards, so tie the rope around yourself and hold on."

...another adventure?

Hiccup soon began to feel much cooler, and after a short time he actually felt very cold.
The little teddy-bear didn't quite understand why it would be cold in Africa.
He looked down and could see the African plains with antelope roaming in their hundreds in the lush grass. He could also see that they were approaching a large hill which soon turned out to be a mountain.
"Where are we?" the cold, shivering teddy-bear asked Algernon.
"We are approaching the highest mountain in Africa. It is called Mount Kilimanjaro."
"Why is it white?" Hiccup called loudly to Algernon.
"It's snow Hiccup. We are very high and the climate is so cold the snow doesn't melt here."
Hiccup soon found out just how cold it was as Algernon flew lower to make a landing in the snow, forgetting that Hiccup might be below him.
Hiccup was below him. Bump; s w o o o o s h !

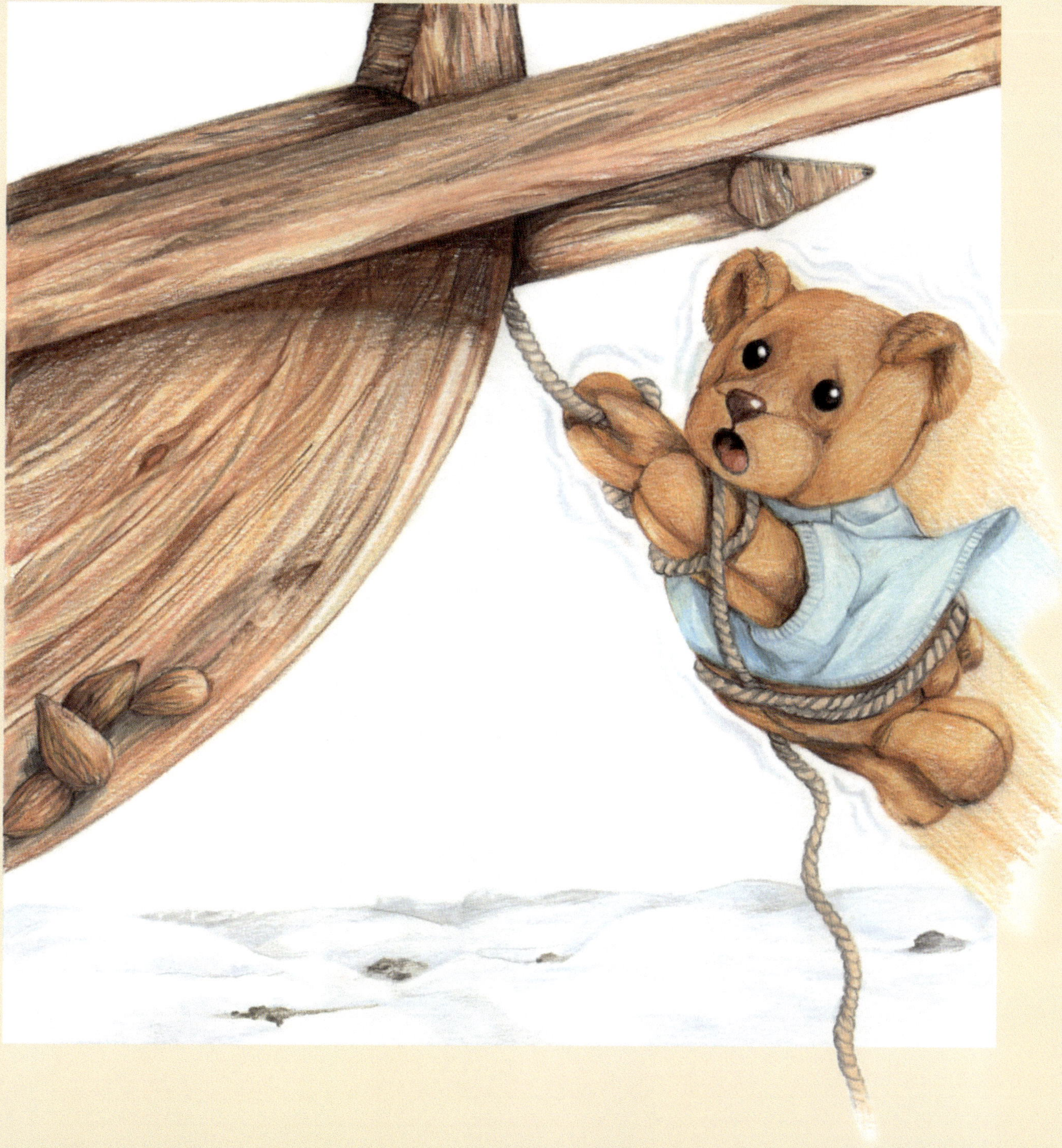

Jumping from his little aeroplane, Algernon was alarmed to see little Hiccup nearly hidden with just his legs showing. He hurried over to help Hiccup.
"Well that took me aback Algernon!" Hiccup said.
"Poor Hiccup!" Algernon was very apologetic for dragging Hiccup through the snow. "I hope that is the end of your troubles now."
"I expect it isn't!" a not-very-happy Hiccup replied.
"Well we are here now, so look around and admire the view, it's awesome, isn't it?" Algernon was proud of his African scenery.
"I'm sure it's lovely but I am still shaking snow from my arms and legs and I liked it when it was warmer." It appeared that Hiccup wouldn't cheer up yet.
"Would you prefer to go somewhere warmer then Hiccup?" Algernon asked him although he would have loved to stay on the mountain for longer.
Then he turned around and noticed that the little aeroplane's wheels had sunk into the snow.

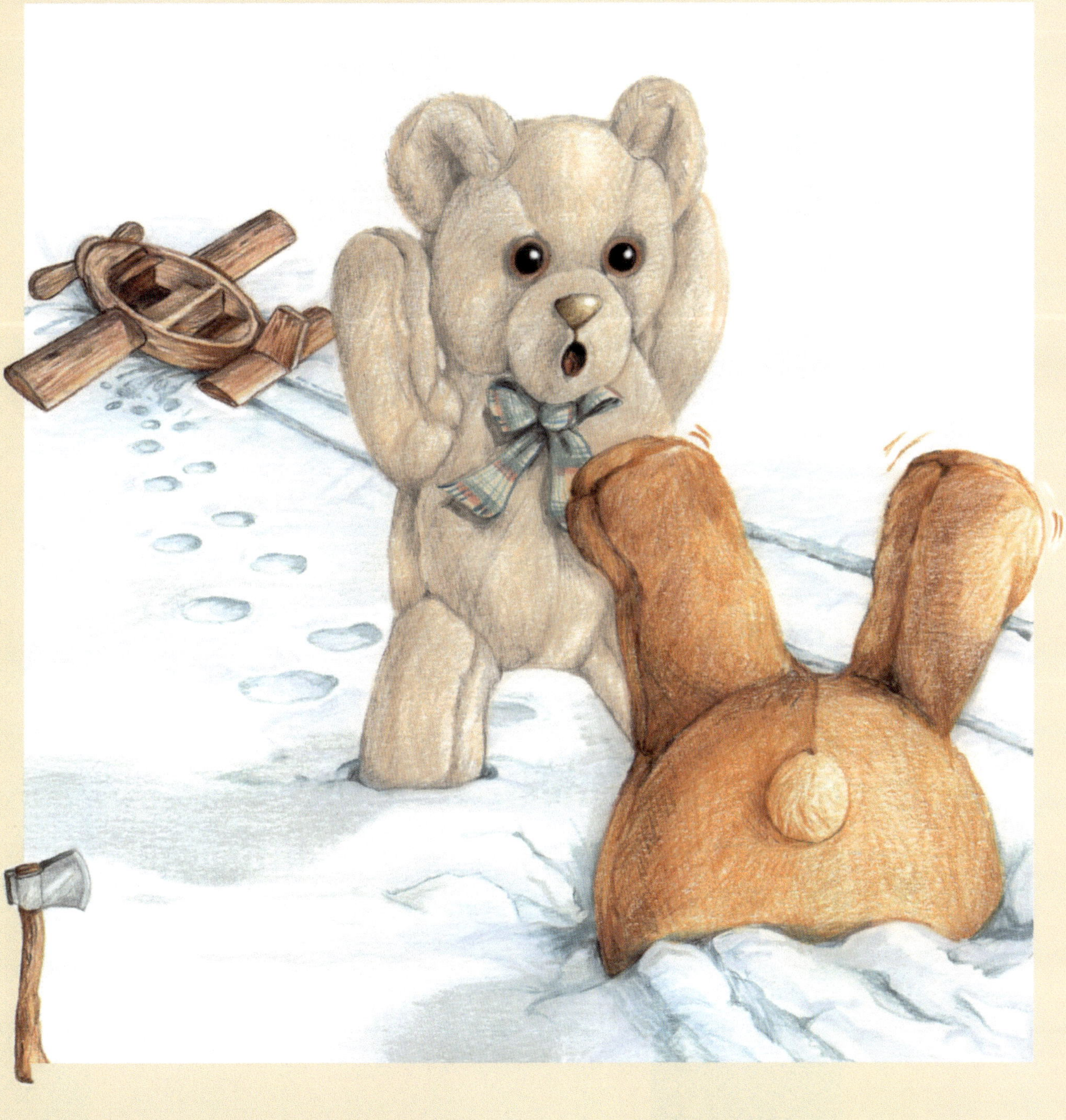

"Oh 'Antsinmypants'." Algernon could see the problem clearly. It was not going to be easy to take off with the wheels firmly stuck in the snow.

"We won't have to stay, will we?" pleaded a cold and unhappy Hiccup.

"No. I think I have a plan. If I sit in the plane and wind the propeller up, you push hard from behind and the aeroplane will skim over the snow and lift off.

Hiccup readied himself for the take-off. He stood at the very back of the little plane. Algernon wound the propeller up and as soon as it was spinning fully, Hiccup began to push.

Slowly it began to move forward, the wheels lifted from the snow and the plane rushed forward. Unfortunately rather faster than either teddy-bear had anticipated.

Rising into the sky above, Algernon flew in his aeroplane.

On the cold snow stood a VERY miserable Hiccup.

...hhmmmph!

Looking up Hiccup called to Algernon as the little aeroplane flew past him.
"What about me?"
The plane had flown right past by this time. On the next fly-past Algernon shouted to Hiccup to grab the tethering rope.
"OK." shouted back Hiccup. "Next time around."
The aeroplane began to fly lower to the ground, tethering rope hanging behind.
Hiccup jumped … and missed. "Next time." he called.
Algernon gave Hiccup a 'thumbs-up' to show he would be ready too.
Down swooped the plane again and Hiccup jumped again and this time he managed to hold on.
Rather than hang on to the rope for a long time, Hiccup pulled himself upward and climbed back into the rear seat behind Algernon.
He settled down for another long flight. He was absolutely exhausted and very soon, fast asleep.

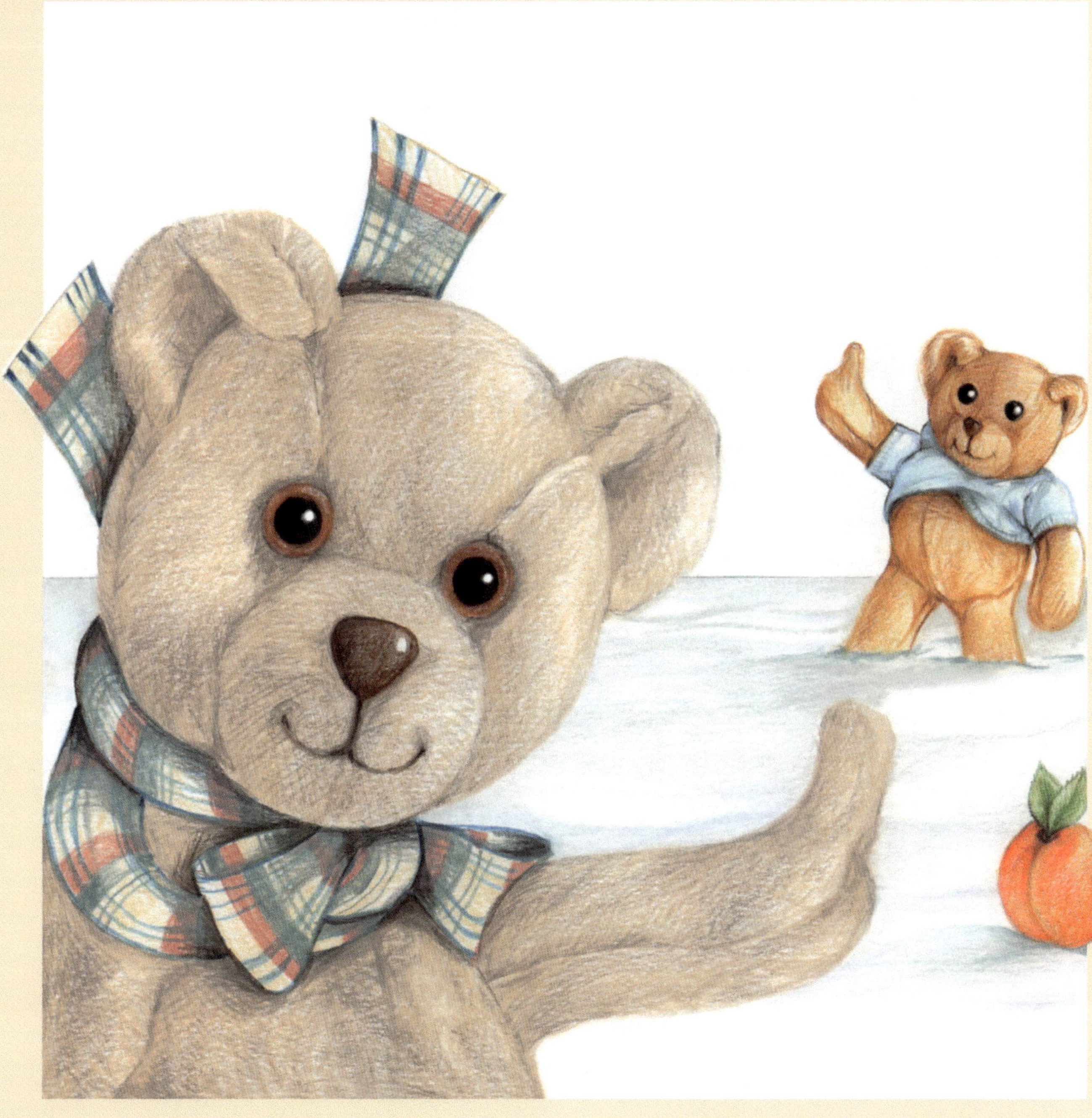

Hiccup awoke to the sound of Algernon saying. "We are here."
"Where is here?" asked Hiccup rubbing his eyes.
"This is Egypt, just look down at the astounding landscape."
"What are the white pointy things?" Hiccup asked.
"Those are the Pyramids, and they are huge." Algernon explained.
"Will we land there?" Hiccup was awake now and actually smiling. This looked like fun.
"Yes we will, but I must warn you about something."
"Oh-ho!" thought Hiccup. "Here, we go! Yes?" he asked.
"Well you remember I told you that this aeroplane was just a bit magical?"
"Mmmm. Yes!" came the reply from Hiccup.
"It is very magical and not only can it fly amazingly quickly but it can travel in time too. I think we have travelled back many years; maybe hundreds of years."
"Yes." replied Hiccup again. "And . . . . ?"

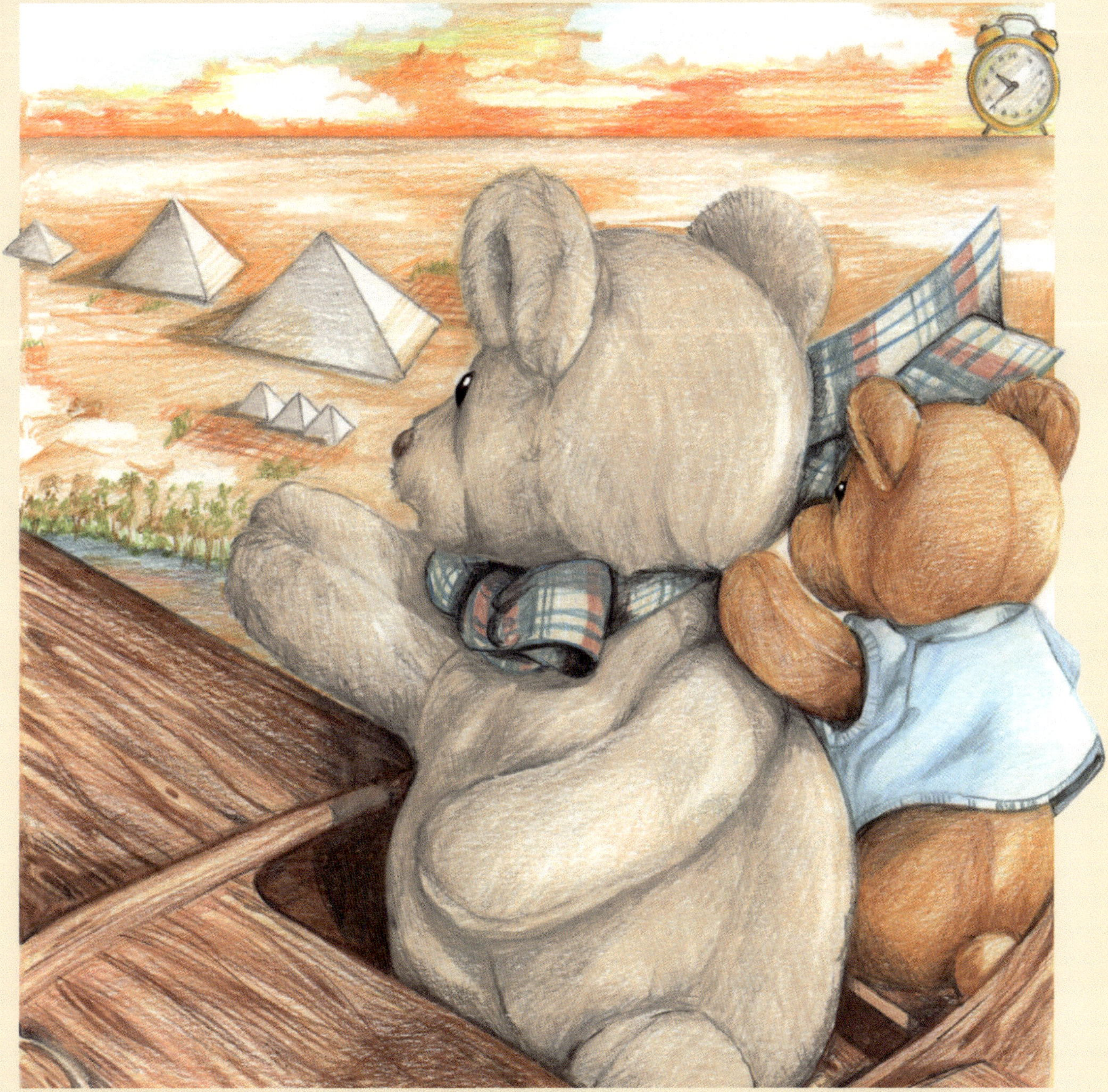

"Well the Pyramids still have their white casing, which in the year we live, has completely disappeared. But it is still here, so we must be in ancient times."

"When I land, I will stop on top of a pyramid, and I want you to throw down the tethering rope, hop out and tie us around the stone top."

"Well that sounds easy." Hiccup told Algernon.

The little plane circled the pyramid and as it lowered onto the top, Hiccup jumped out, grabbed the rope and tied it tightly to the top around one of the shiny white polished blocks. But not tightly enough.

Now, of course, the aeroplane was hanging down the slope of the pyramid. Algernon hopped out to join Hiccup. As soon as he stood on the stone blocks he slipped and held on to the only thing he could . . . the aeroplane. That also began sliding and finally behind the aeroplane followed Hiccup who was still holding tightly to the rope.

Down they slid, from the very top to the lowest point on the ground – it was a very long way!

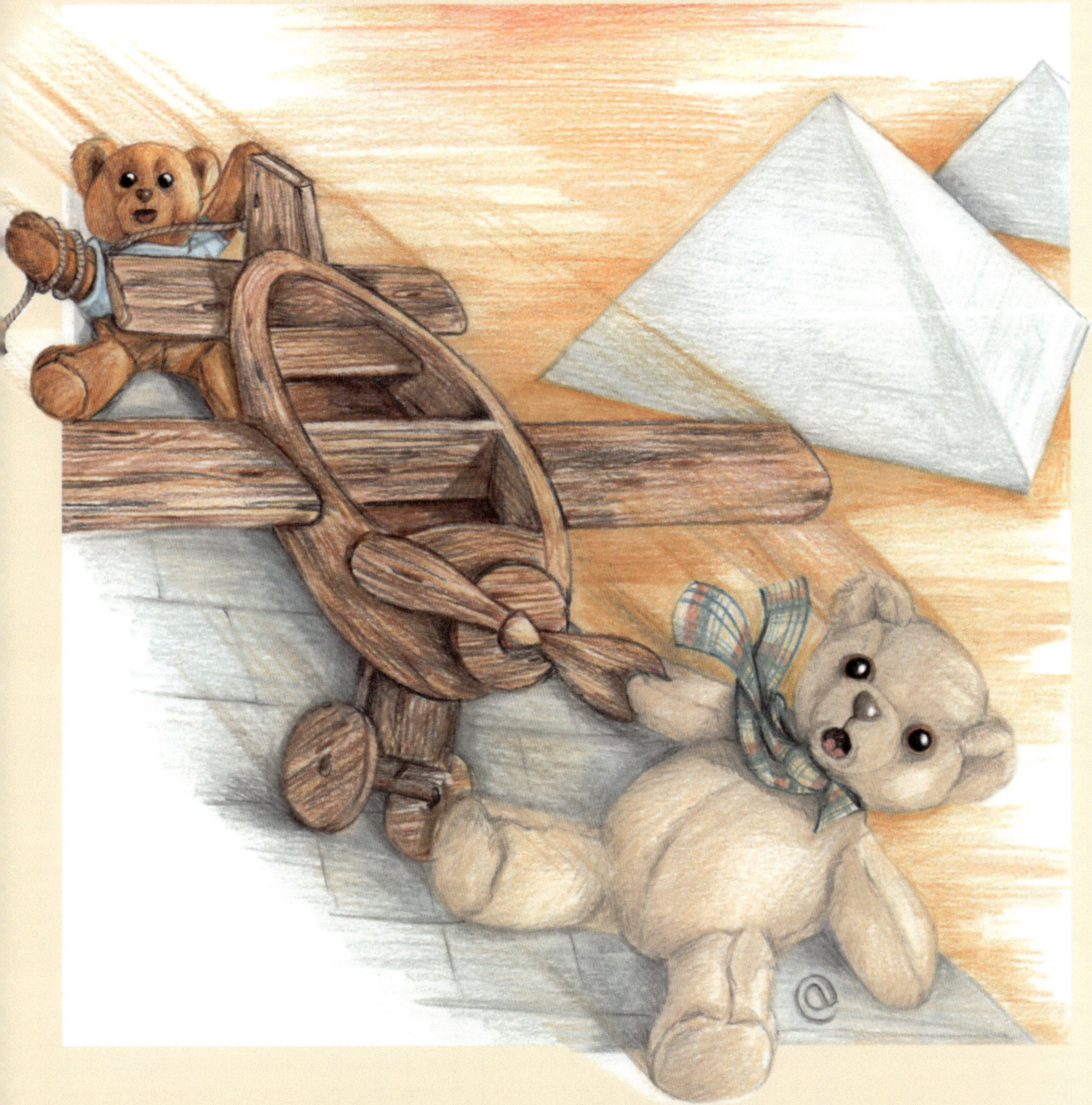

The tangled heap of aeroplane, Hiccup and Algernon began to sort itself out.

Hiccup arose first.

"Now you see what I mean, Algernon, about always finding trouble. Or rather trouble always finding me?"

Looking around the two teddy-bears were amazed to spot a huge lion-like 'something' nearby. There didn't appear to be any people or any teddy-bears so they wandered over to the 'lion-thing'. Getting close they realised that it was an attractive stone sculpture. It was made to resemble a lion but with human's head and long lion-like body. Hiccup stretched up but couldn't even reach the the top of one of the blocks of the 'lion-thing's' paw. It was really huge.

The 'Lion-thing' was actually 'The Great Sphinx of Giza' which has been near the Pyramids in Egypt for thousands of years.

...look Algernon!

"It's very hot here Algernon." Hiccup complained.
"Are you saying that you want to leave already?"
"Well perhaps we could very soon. It is a lot for one tiny teddy-bear to do in one day, isn't it?"
But Algernon was looking hard at the 'lion-thing' and remembered something he had been told.
"We must be at the site of the Great Egyptian Pyramids and this must be 'The Sphinx'. Look closely Hiccup and see if you can spot a doorway in the side of the Sphinx? There should be several."
It was Hiccup who found a little stone doorway set at the back and he was even able to move the stone in front of it. Algernon was soon by his side.
"I hope the aeroplane's magic works here." he told Hiccup.
"Then we can ask to be taken to Brazil in South America." Algernon's face lit up as he said this.
"Then you can meet another teddy-bear who is Bruno. He lives in Brazil, in the rainforest. It would be a lovely way to continue your travels."

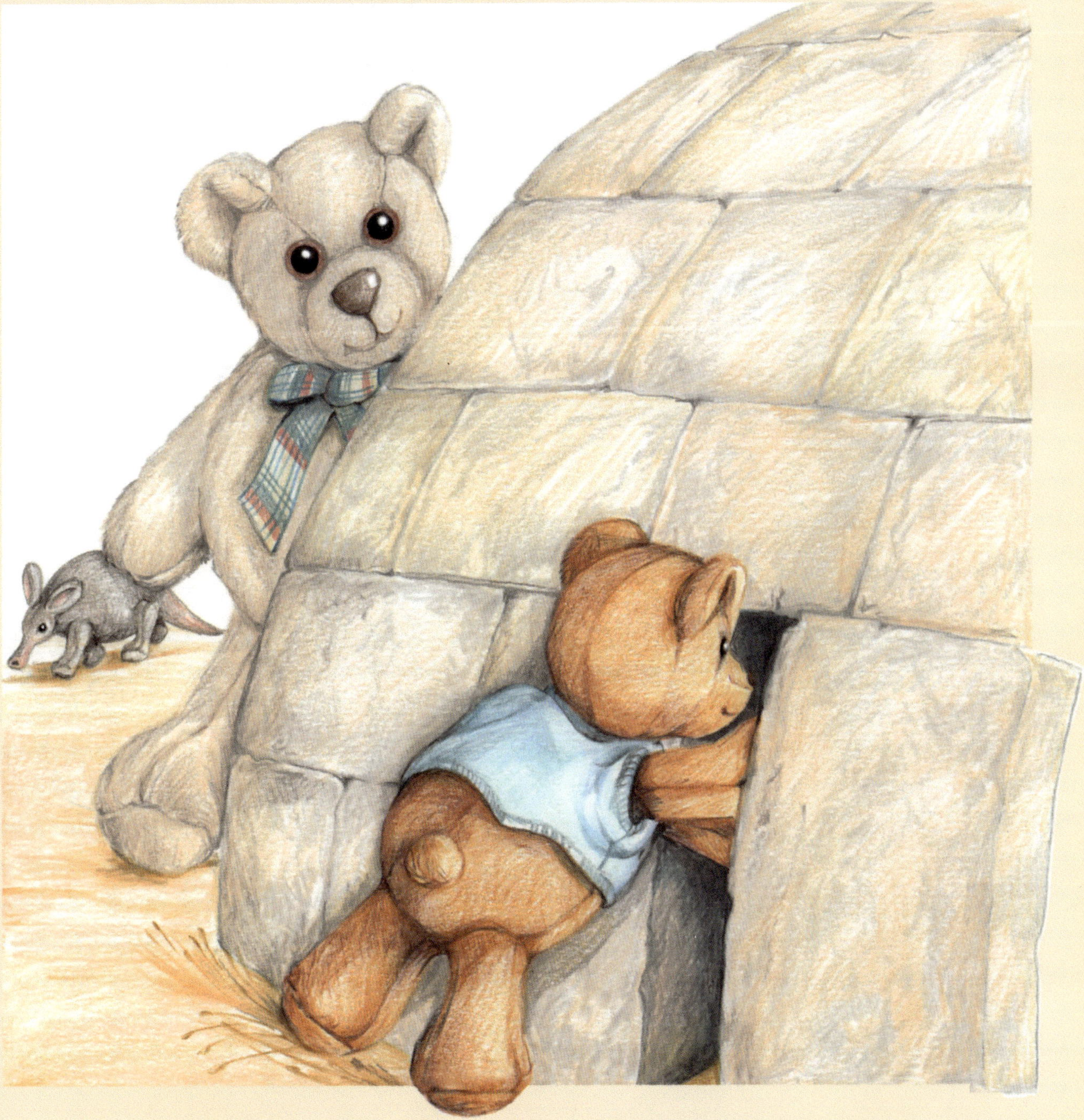

Hiccup stepped through the doorway and realised he was leaving Africa and going to South America. He smiled and told Algernon. "I have just thought. The two continents we have visited both start and end with the letter 'A'."

"Yes they do and do you know what else? Apart from Europe all the other continents also start and end with the letter 'A'. There are Asia, Australasia and Antarctica as well as Africa and America"

Hiccup was more interested in where he was going now. "Are you sure this is the way Algernon?"

"Oh yes. Don't worry Hiccup. Just follow the tunnel."

"What will happen to your amazing aeroplane?" Hiccup seemed anxious.

"Oh don't worry. I will let you go to meet Bruno and I will go back and check that it's alright, then I can fly away."

"And then?" asked Hiccup.

"Then I can have more adventures in my Amazing Aeroplane."

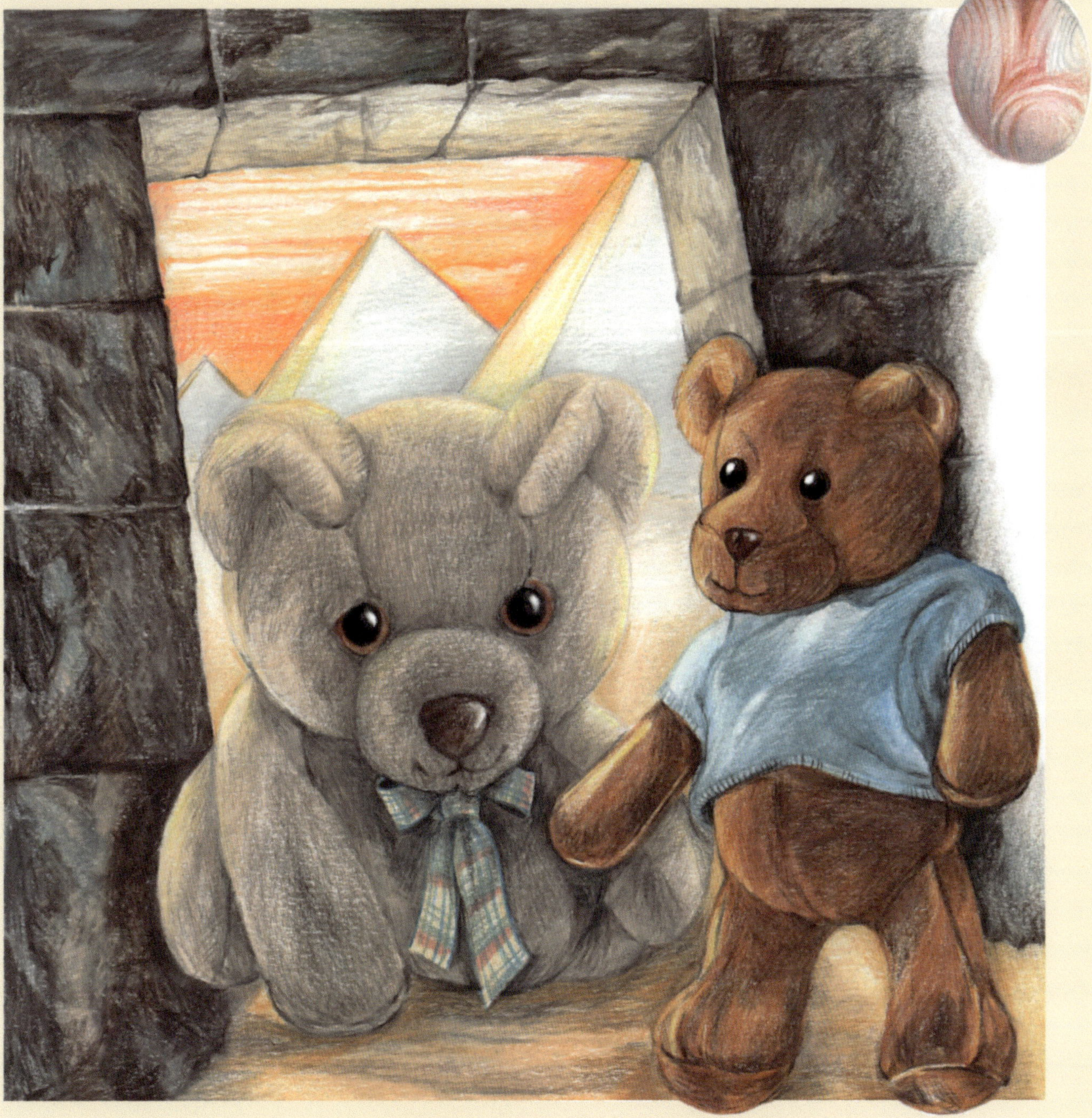

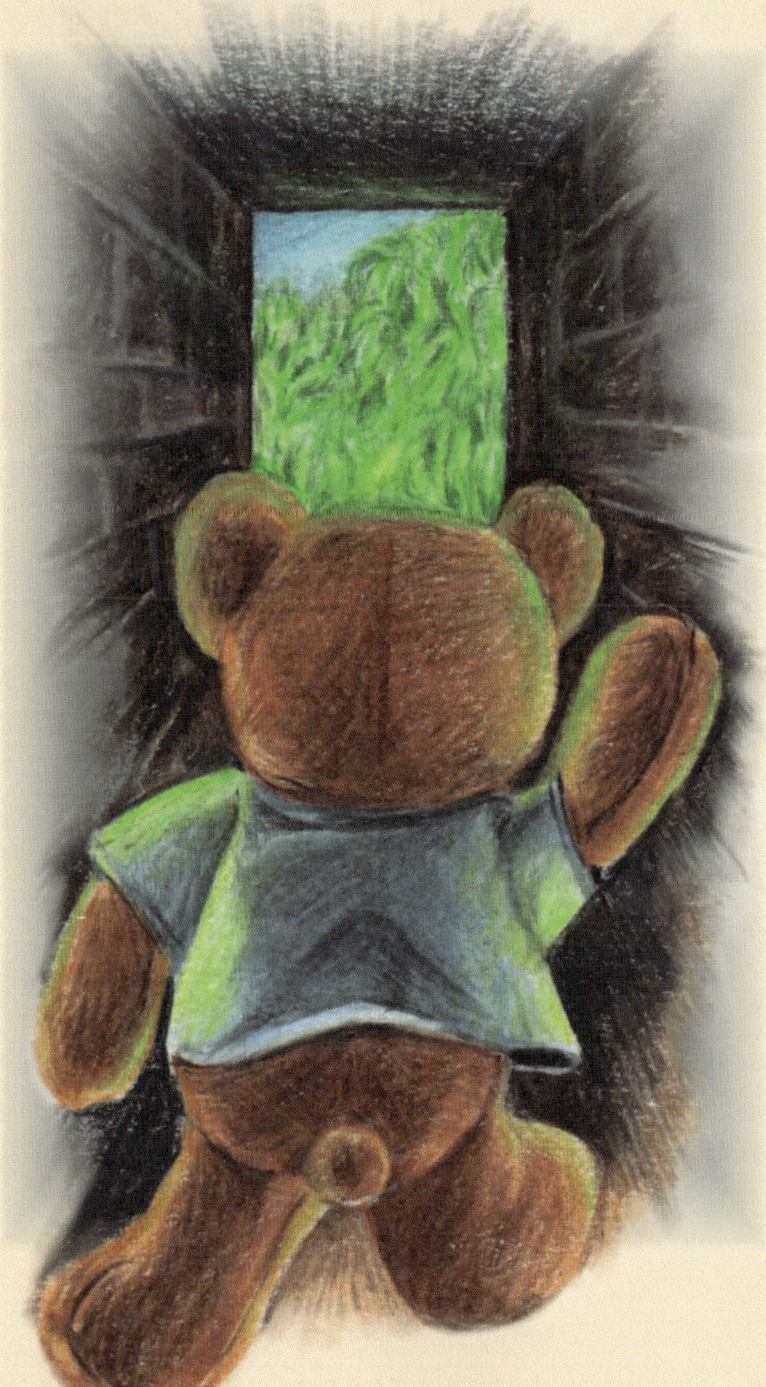

Well, did you find the things beginning with the letter 'A'?
In the first main picture you may have seen:

apples

asparagus

arrow

atom

ampersand ('and' symbol)

ant

antelope (Gemsbok)

albatross

almonds

axe

anchor

apricot

alarm clock

'at'symbol

avocado pear

ardvaark

agate

If you enjoyed the story of Algernon and Hiccup, in the next story the Alphabet begins again with 'B'.
Hiccup meets Bruno in Brazil.

The Alphabetical list of story titles.

Algernon and his Amazing Aeroplane
Bruno in the Brazilian Rainforest
Chomondley's Circus
Dreyfus the Dreamer
Extraordinary Edward and the Easy 'E's
Fabulous Fionora's Magic Feather
Galileo and his Goodness Gracious Goggles
Harry and Hiccup play Hide & Seek
Ivan and his Ice Cream Van
Jemima Juggling Jelly beans
Katy at Keeper's Cottage in Kimmeridge
Lulworth and his Liquorice Laboratory
Manuel and his Marvellous Minis
Nimbus and his Nine Number puzzles
Ophelia the Opera singer
Pierre the Paris Painter
Quinn's Quirky Quicksilver
Ria's Riddles and Puzzles
Scrap in the Swiss Snow
Teddy Bear's Tricky Toyshop
Umberto and his Umber Umbrella
Victoria's Vanishing Room
Whisper the nearly Wonder Wizard
Xaviar and the Extraordinary 'X'
Yaffle and his Yellow Yacht
Zak and his Zooming Zeppelin

Algernon	Bruno	Chomondeley	Dreyfus	Edward	Fionora	Galileo
Harry	Ivan	Jemima	Katy	Lulworth	Manuel	Nimbus
Ophelia	Pierre	Quinn	Ria	Scrap	Teddy	
Umberto	Victoria	Whisper	Xaviar	Yaffle	Zak	

Alpha Beta Bears

...and of course Hiccup.

'Next, it's my story,'
said Bruno.

Printed in Great Britain
by Amazon